ANOTHER DAY

ANOTHER CHALLENGE

Every morning, as Albert Crunkle's mother got up from the breakfast table, she would say, "Oh well, another day, another challenge."

That was how Albert Crunkle came to grow up looking for challenges. He looked every day for something he could do that would be bigger or brighter or bolder than what he had done yesterday.

"I've been brought up like that, you see," he told his wife, Adeline, as he kissed her and the children goodbye each morning.

3

He climbed the highest mountain in the country.
He ate more apples in one sitting than anyone had before.
He gathered the largest collection of tropical fish that had
ever been kept in one tank. "Albert Crunkle, the record-
breaker, has done it again!" said the newspapers almost
every week.

He held his breath under water
longer than anyone ever had.

He sat in a snakepit with 75 snakes for a whole night.
He pushed a wheelbarrow all the way across a desert.

"Of course, I do get rather tired of being noticed," said Albert Crunkle to his wife one evening. "It's very hard work being famous, you know. Sometimes I wish I did ordinary things."

But he went on looking for more challenges — and found them.

He sat up on a pole for a whole week.

He crossed a raging river on a tightrope.

He spent a month in a cave living only on vegetables.

Albert's name was in every record book.

"It's getting quite difficult to find a new challenge," said Albert.

"I can offer you one," said Adeline. "Cook the dinner while I take the children to buy some new shoes."

"That's hardly a challenge," said Albert.

But it was.

"I've never had to climb a mountain twice to get it right, but I think I'll have to try this again," said Albert Crunkle. So he sent Adeline off on a drive in the country while he practiced cooking the dinner again.

"I'd like to try a bit of mountain-climbing," said Adeline later that evening. "Would you look after the children while I give it a try? I promise you it will be a challenge."

And it was.

"I think I should try that again," said Albert Crunkle.

So Adeline went off to run a marathon. Adeline came first in the marathon. She won a trophy.

The next morning, Adeline kissed Albert and the children good-bye and went off to do something not even Albert had ever done. She was going to sit on the bottom of the sea in a cage for a week.

"Have a nice time, dear," said Albert. "I'm sure you'll find it very peaceful watching the fish."

The next week she went hang gliding. She flew a longer distance than anyone had ever flown.

Then she tried juggling. She was the best juggler the town had ever seen.

Adeline was being noticed a lot. Adeline was becoming famous.

"You're right, Albert," said Adeline one evening. "It is quite hard work being famous."

"Hard work!" said Albert. "You should try doing ordinary things. That's hard work."

"I've tried that," said Adeline. "I think I prefer being famous."

Albert Crunkle sat down to breakfast with the children.
"Oh well, another day, another challenge," he said.

And it was.